Explosion of the Dreams Deferred

Riva Figueroa

Presentation by *BookLeaf Publishing*

Web: www.bookleafpub.com

E-mail: info@bookleafpub.com

ISBN: 9789357612999

First edition 2022

*For Daddy, a wolf whispering wisdom and
mischief in my ear*

Cotton Candy Sky

Thinking of you under the cotton candy sky

So many sweet possibilities sinking into twilight
on the night air

Reactions

Lust like a soft breeze
Ripples over skin like lake water
Soft lapping at shore wetly
River rocks shining shifting
The smallest of rocking releasing
The ebb and flow of longing
Rides passion of remembered touch
Of ecstasy
I miss your body
There are too many words
In the spaces between our touches

Tell Them You Love Them

I don't even know how many years it's been
since daddy died

But I'll tell you I did just burst into tears
realizing that well I had to tell a lover I loved
him

the why of why I had to tell him speared my
heart.

sometimes you don't get 20 years.

sometimes you don't get enough time with for
love and even if you do is it ever going to feel
like it was enough and sometimes you get a call
that someone's gonna live two months and so
then you suck the marrow out of life all the
moments possible for four years and then you
get a call in the middle of the night and you were
planning to go home in eight weeks and they're
gone the last thing you texted them as I love you
and they said I can't wait to see you.

So i tell people i love them when i love them

Little Bits

I fall for you
I catch myself
I tell myself
It is ok
Like falling asleep
And startling awake
Little falls
It it ok I tell myself
I am only a little bit sleepy
I am only a little bit
endlessly bit by little bit
Falling in love

How Many Moons

As the moon sheds from peak
Waves ebb to shore
I cannot stop the crashing

A whispering

In the foam
In the receeding

The wreckage

How many people do you need to have tell you
they love you before you feel loved enough?

For you it is never enough

I am never enough

And yet I am too much

An ocean

Ebb and flow

Endlessly moving

The moon smiling knowingly as she watches my
tears hopes dreams inner tsunami move in love
as she cycles light to dark

She and I endlessly dance to the same music, my
sister in the sky, the goddess, the priestess, this
ageless sensual sofia

Ah but you

She laughs at your longing

You are never ready

And you have never learned to swim

Dip limbs in water and call it love then

Fly away and no, it will never be enough

Where Water Remembers

Run away with me to a place where bridges do
not go

Where rocks tumble into roads and the world
pauses

Where I pause too and know not the meaning of
Mondays

Look into my eyes

Let me feel your joy
Let me taste your laughter in the air
Let your awe whistle in the tall grass

Something whispered here and the current
carried it away but the echo of it ripples in my
heart

I hear your heart skip with it
Look into my eyes and tell me your heart does
not skip
There was a sacred valley once

Far down where only the water knows our
names

I have left a bit of my soul there
Run away with me
Let's find it together

Pachamama Smile

My home this place
It lights me up inside
They say I have a beautiful smile
It is hers though, my Pachamama
I share it
This is my mother shining through me
Glowing
So alive
Pachamama in all her grace
The sky hat on her head
Hilltops and mountains her curves
The joy of her shining through me
Singing daydream lullabies of possibility
I want to dance mama
Just over that hill
I smile
I hear you calling…

Lovers on the Dance Floor

I have lost myself in this moment
In your arms love
Pressed together
Swaying
There is color music laughter
A room a life a sense of wonder
I am blind to all this but you
You
Being here with me
The sound I hear is our heartbeats
Someone will tell me later it was a drum
But I think love
It was us

Potato Poem

When you feel tired of life let me show you my
joys
They are infinite and varied like the colors and
shapes of the potatoes in my home country
They are soft and fluffy as the silkiest baby
alpaca
They have an untranslatable humorous wisdom
as does this llama tolerating photography on the
streets of Cusco, rainbow fabric bits as her decor
Let me show you all the things that light me up
inside that give me joy that nourish my soul
Joy sprout up with red shiny purple green leaves
Joy cuddles close and happy
Joy has ancient stories to tell
Let us hear them
This earth has endless joy to offer us if only you
listen and watch

Don't Tempt Me

Don't Tempt Me

"I need someone to help me go deep"
Don't tempt me.

Lust hangs on the air between us
I can taste the sticky with my tongue
It is soft and silky warm and I want it
I feel my body's response
And I dwell in it

Don't tempt me

My energy shifts and I want to curl into you and
dive
This is not shallow water
This is energy like ocean
This is lighthouses and tidal waves
Surf and salt spray
This is air whipped to frenzy
And deep blue rooted truth

The way you move your body
Fascinates mine

Don't tempt me

I stand so still
My breath pauses
My thoughts pause
I am awash in sensation

It is both a curse and a blessing to feel
everything so deeply
It is in knowing sensing pleasure as yet unmet
and oh perhaps never met is there in this meeting
It is not longing as much as an acknowledging
This then is the body in its wanting
And
Perhaps I had forgotten
Perhaps again this is a new way of sensing

Don't tempt me

Your eyes on me
Mine go downcast
Meet yours again
Smile
Blush

My eyes signal interest
I cannot stop them
They have decided to open the windows of my
soul
Dialate as the heart palpitates

I skip a beat
I stumble
I say too many words
I blush
The energy of the oceans I contain the
multitudinous of emotion in me… suddenly
flows focused on you

I may never send you these thoughts
We may never go this depth
Inside me though the ache is there though

The temptation
The lust on air

"You each have my number, just putting it out
there."

Don't tempt me.

Only the Night Knows

And there are some things only the night knows

She buries that knowing deeply away, next to
longing, next to wishing connection was like
lightning across the night sky.

Clear. Just for a moment. So clear.

There are days it whispers into the sunrise. A
cloud wisp of promise as dewily draped as the
spidersweb. A pulse on air as fast and throbbing
as the blue bellied hummingbird.

She prays the afternoon will understand, forgive
the terribly innocent temptations of morning,
hold gently ponder softly the flowing
temptations singing at night.

Dissolve

There is delight ahead as yet unmet
The sense of it intoxicates, excites, ignites
So big and oh so unknown
So better in some indescribable way of all things
before in this life
In work in love in moments of far reaching bliss
so deep so high so very everything
I am in awe of the knowing of that
Too knowing not how go there I
Just that I go
Alit moment by moment
Ahhh this then is the next right thing

Perhaps
You
You a thing
Who knew

Ahh delight me as yet untravelled you, wander
dance sing move play the music this path song
Feed our souls

Slow down
Sink

Melt
Summers heat radiates
Give me a cold drink
Sit here with me
So close and not yet touching
I can't wait to get you into a room with AIR
CONDITIONING
Watch tiny hairs stand on end electric
The air there like this ice I slow sip
Dissolve on tongue
Just as you will

Balcony Problems

"The fact that I am not lounging naked on the
balcony… Quite frankly it's problematic"…

My answer to that
oh darling bloom where planted
petrichor in the air
monsoons are coming
a few weeks away the deluge

yet this morning though
and the one before the one to come
cloudscape and hummingbird song
air caressing exposed skin

nary a problem to be present to
it feels good
no island needed

Magic

When you said
But I do believe in magic
Well
You should
You are

Music Echo Suspended Desire

I like the smell of you on my skin. I am warm. The air of the fan above is cool. From my skin the scent of you is rising from my heart where I had been pressed into you, and I am intoxicated by this, a smoky masculine scent and ooh it is good, these sensations are so good.

It feels now in my body like I'm vibrating with the energy and echo of our wanting, of temptation as if vibration as if string played and the memory of music is an echo suspended, desire.

Want

You said I make you feel so wanted.

You are

I am laying abed

Wanting you
still
again
more

Wanting like a liquid gold luscious lust moving
along my hips, my heart, my mind.

Wanton.

So yes. Feel wanted.

You are.

Pear Tree

I have done yoga in misty cool air under the
patio pear tree two mornings now.

The ants do not bite. Big ants and little ants of
two colonies sent their scouts to explore me. I
am not a pear. They tickle me anyway.

A bee tried to get inside my pants. In through
lattice on the side. Down through the emerald
ring in my belly. Daring bee, to seek such
intimacy. I do all I can not to harm it. It is
determined to dive deep into me and I feel it
vibrating soft black and yellow bits of
curiousity, refusing to be safely still. I paused.
Laughingly blew it away, a gentle kiss on air,
listen to its soft buzz. Twice. Smile softly at that.
It is always lovely to be mistaken for a flower.
Twice.

Moving feels like honey. I am so very happy in
this here. This now. I am so open in this wet
green place.

I glean the unripe fallen pears from the stones.
Bruised. Edible if I work with them properly.

Poached honey lavendar pear in a pot slow
simmers on the stove.

The day moves, grey to sun, ever shifting and
still itself.

As do I.

Secret Garden

Secret gardens, yet too the magic of those that are not secret but grow on streets on walls, the growing greenly energy, everywhere so magic, of dropping into moments, even wandering city streets, we are present to see it, let ourselves feel it. The garden theme carried through into a cafe, whose wraps clearly flirted, wanting to be tasted. Romantic and a Hot & Healthy Bachelor indeed, with words everywhere like "celebrating the energy of healing", (the Hot & Healthy Bachelor is the green filled wrap) and then, Joni Mitchell reminding us to get back in the garden, and that we are stardust, and golden

All the things that light me up inside, and indeed, my joys felt like green ivy unfurling, dancing along through bricks and cobblestones. Simple, and somehow defiant, a secret public garden.

A Morning Poem

think of you upon waking

again

what is it you do to me
all this so much and not yet done has us undone

waking
wanting

full with wonder and a touch of lust

again

In Orchard, Smitten

I am in the apple orchard/smitten by this New
England fall

the cool clear air

Mist and promise by morning

A midday sun and I too glow

A ladder to reach the heights I dream of and step
back down to earth as needed

Sweet and hard as is life as are many good
things

Leave change color and fruit falls

As do I
Oh as do I

Light Up Heart

He has a little heart in on a white bookshelf

He made it himself
It lights up when he flicks the switch
Turns it on

Just like me
Just like him too
Turned on
Lit up
Flickering with light

I lay abed at night still flickering
Images of a light up heart
Images of him

His heart with its light up parts and soft circuits,
shown to me, remains safely shelved in its
cubby.

When whats right for him is right and meant to
happen, it will happen.

Soft circuits
Plastic boxes
Boxes of parts

Labels and systems everywhere

White cubbies and everything shelved

Waiting